Little Bean

Jonathan Shaw

Primix Publishing
11620 Wilshire Blvd
Suite 900, West Wilshire Center, Los Angeles, CA, 90025
www.primixpublishing.com
Phone: 1-800-538-5788

© 2021 Jonathan Shaw. All rights reserved.

No part of this book may be reproduced, stored in a retrieval system, or transmitted by any means without the written permission of the author.

Published by Primix Publishing   08/12/2021

ISBN: 978-1-955177-29-0(sc)
ISBN: 978-1-955177-30-6(e)

Library of Congress Control Number: 2021913610

Any people depicted in stock imagery provided by iStock are models, and such images are being used for illustrative purposes only.

Certain stock imagery © iStock.

Because of the dynamic nature of the Internet, any web addresses or links contained in this book may have changed since publication and may no longer be valid. The views expressed in this work are solely those of the author and do not necessarily reflect the views of the publisher, and the publisher hereby disclaims any responsibility for them.

Little Bean

Little bean is a little girl who really loves to… DREAM

Mom and dad tells little bean that she can be ANYTHING

So little bean dreams

of being an angel with

GOLDEN wings

Little bean also dreams
that she's a QUEEN
of everything

Little bean Dreams and
Dreams. She's a supermodel
on **MAGAZINES**

Even when she's not asleep little bean still believes that she can do ANYTHING

Little bean can overcome all
IMPOSSIBILITIES

Nothing **EVER** holds little **BEAN BACK** she'll keep believing and that's a **FACT**

So little bean DREAMS
BELIEVES
And even does one more thing

Little bean hope's that you know that you can dream too!

www.ingramcontent.com/pod-product-compliance
Lightning Source LLC
Chambersburg PA
CBHW061108070526
44579CB00011B/182